# Castles in the Sand

# Castles in the Sand

Created by
MICHAEL DIPERSIO

Text by
JEFFREY SHEAR & STEVEN SCHNEIDER

Photography by
TOBY RICHARDS

A Mountain Lion Book

A PERIGEE BOOK

Perigee Books
are published by
G. P. Putnam's Sons
200 Madison Avenue
New York, New York 10016

Library of Congress Cataloging in Publication Data

DiPersio, Michael.
    Castles in the sand.

    "A Perigee book."
    1. Sand craft.   2. Sandcastles.   I. Shear, Jeff.
II. Richards, Toby. III. Title.
TT865.D56 1982      736'.9       81-17914
ISBN 0-399-50599-7          AACR2

First Perigee printing, 1982
Printed in the United States of America

Designed by *Dilip Kane*     Illustrated by *Maryann Lis*     Typography by *TypeHouse of Pennington, Pennington, NJ*

# Table of Contents

1  Before You Begin                          1

2  The Fantasy Castle                        5

3  A Lighthouse by the Sea                  29

4  The Alamo                                35

5  The Ponte Vecchio                        43

6  The Colosseum                            49

7  The Eiffel Tower                         57

8  Great Wall of China                      65

9  The Great Pyramid of Giza                71

10  The Capitol                             75

11  The White House                         81

12  Sand Drippings                          89

13  Photographing Sandcastles              93

14  How to Enter a Sandcastle Contest      99

# Acknowledgments

We would like to thank Laurisa Kane for her accurate manuscript typing; Connie Kellner, Maryann Perrine, and Leslie Cahill of The TypeHouse of Pennington for their precise workmanship and for caring; John Monteleone of Mountain Lion Books and Sam Mitnick of Perigee Books for believing; and the Atlantic City Weatherman for cooperating when we needed sunshine and blue skies.

# Introduction

This is a different kind of book on sandcastles. If you've only got an hour to spare, this book will show you how to build a complete castle, start to finish, step by step, in one hour, even if it's the first time you try. If you feel more ambitious, we've provided a project you can build from start to finish in two hours. And if you're interested in a "sunburn special," you can end your day at the beach with a dazzling castle.

First, you'll build a fantasy castle which will teach you all the fundamentals of sandcastle construction. If you practice these basic techniques, you'll be able to build any castle or structure you want. If you never built a castle before, this book will show you how to progress from beginner to expert.

Each "castle" (we've used the term loosely in order to include some famous landmarks) has its own set of building instructions and a brief profile of the structure you're remaking in sand. By the time you work your way through the book, you'll be able to build famous structures such as the Colosseum and Eiffel Tower.

*Castles in the Sand* is a book to take with you to the beach. We've included information on How to Enter a Sandcastle Contest and Photographing Sandcastles because we expect you will be making some super castles—ones that you'll want to capture in photographs before wind and water wash them away.

A really good sandcastle always attracts onlookers and admirers. We've had many interesting conversations with people who just happened to walk by and ask what in the world we were doing. So be prepared to meet new friends as well as to have a lot of fun.

# Castles in the Sand

# 1 Before You Begin

## Tides

The trick to building a good sandcastle is learning something about the tides. I have learned to start working one or two hours after high tide, because then the sand you use to build your pile will be wet from the outgoing tide. Damp, well-packed sand is the basis of all good sandcastle construction. Thus, check your local newspaper for high- and low-tide listings. These are usually printed alongside the weather report. If you are a landlubber, the tides may be mysterious at first, but soon you will discover that they are always on time.

Another important reason for starting to build an hour or so after high tide is to avoid getting washed away—especially if you want to build an ambitious project—since you'll have as many as eight to ten hours before the tide returns to the level where you started.

Once you have determined the best time to start working, you will need to select an area of the beach that will most readily lend itself to the work at hand. Try to find a spot where the sand is not too pebbly or coarse.

A smooth, fine sand will hold together well when it is packed. Stones, seashells, and pebbles all tend to coarsen your sand and create problems. There is nothing more disappointing than seeing a tower crumble because of an unseen shell buried in the sand. Spend some time combing the beach for a place where the sand is good; you'll have an easier time building your sandcastle. Never be too hasty in selecting a location. Well begun is half-done, and once you have found a good spot, you may want to return to it again and again.

Remember—the time of day you begin your castle will determine how much time you have to work on it. If you start an hour or two after high tide, you will have until the next high tide to finish your castle, usually about eight to ten hours. If the high tide is at eight o'clock in the morning and you don't get out to the beach until noon, keep in mind that you'll have about six hours to finish before the water washes your work away.

## The Elements

### The Sun

The sun is both friend and foe to the sandcastler. On occasion the sun will dry out the sand to create a very desirable effect. For example, the sides of the Great Pyramid look better in sand after they have been baked out for a while. On the other hand, the sun can dry out a tower or the side of a wall before you finish the entire castle. Drying may even cause some crumbling or a fatal collapse. You can avoid this by always beginning your work with well-packed, moist sand. If you do, your castle should withstand even the hottest sun.

Building sandcastles is a great way to get a tan and a fantastic way to relax, but don't spoil the fun by getting too much sun. Be sure to protect against sunburn. Long hours on the beach building a sandcastle or even just one hour exposed to too much sunlight can be painful. Use a protective suntan lotion or oil; wear a T-shirt. A visor or sun hat is good to bring along when you are going to be out on the beach for very long.

### Rain

Even the most avid sandcastle builders stay off the beach during rainstorms. Anything more than a light summer rain will make it difficult for walls and turrets to hold. And for the sandcastler, a light rain even has advantages. One really good thing about working in a light rain is that most people are off the beach. As long as you don't mind getting wet, you can work through a light rain. There will be no distractions, and many castlers prefer the solitude of a near-deserted beach. Another advantage to working in a light summer rain is that your sand will remain damp and workable. I once built the Ponte Vecchio on a drizzly, cloudy afternoon. When it came time to put in the archways of the bridge, I had no trouble because the sand stayed just wet enough to remain firm and prevent any caving in.

### The People/Pet Problem

Towers and bridges are particularly vulnerable to kids and Frisbees. Ask anyone playing Frisbee or catch to move down the beach. Explain to them that you don't want a Frisbee gliding through the midsection of your tower or a beach ball landing on one of your bridges. Even innocent bystanders pose a problem. Be sure to keep a lookout so that admiring observers don't get too close to your working area. One misplaced foot can bring down the Eiffel Tower!

Unwitting joggers can also cause catastrophes. If it's a crowded day and your castle seems threatened, plant some stakes and square off an area large enough for you to build comfortably.

The first time I ever built the Colosseum I had to contend with a frisky dog who kept running up to my pile and sniffing it. I was afraid that on one of his visits, he might run through the side of the Colosseum. Although

he didn't, he did manage to use my facsimile of the great Roman arena instead of a tree.

One last bit of advice. Sand crabs tend to burrow in the sand and often find their way into the pile unexpectedly. As you use the sand from your pile, you may unwittingly build a wall in which a sand crab has buried itself. There is a very real danger that the escaping sand crab's vibrations may bring down an entire wall. While you are gathering sand for your pile, look out for them. These sand creatures are harmless—except to would-be architects.

### The Sea

There's not much you can do about the inevitable. Eventually the tide comes in and washes away your castle. But by then you should have a super castle, one that will have attracted many admirers. You may want to photograph your castle as the waves slowly wash it away. (See Chapter 13, Photographing Sandcastles, for some suggestions).

So much for the vicissitudes of life. Post a guard if you want to go for a swim. Take shifts sculpting, guarding, and swimming. That way everyone stays cool, the castle stays up, and everyone gets the joy of working on it.

## The Tools

Most of the tools you'll need to build your sandcastles can be found around the house. You'll find that buckets and smaller cups and cones will be ideal for making molds. Special tools, like a spatula, will

come in handy for carving a variety of shapes from your molds. A melon baller is the sandcastler's favorite for decorating ledges.

The list that follows includes all the tools you'll need to build the ten different structures in this book. Many of them will not be needed every time you go to the beach. The yardstick, for example, only comes in handy for building the pyramid. Check the lists at the beginning of each castle to see which ones you'll need for that structure.

General tools:

- shovel or spade
- hand shovel
- plastic beach pail or bucket, 8 to 10 inches in diameter
- plastic cup, 4 to 6 inches in diameter
- funnel
- 6-inch metal or plastic ruler
- 12-inch metal or plastic ruler
- spatula (the kind used for frosting cakes)

Special tools:

- melon baller
- yardstick
- flat board, 3 feet by 6 inches
- plastic-stem wineglass
- flowerpot
- popcorn bowl
- single-edge razor blade

Of course, you may not always come to the beach prepared to build a sandcastle. Sometimes you just start building a castle spontaneously. When you do, you've got to improvise. Your hands make the best tools, but pieces of stray driftwood, sharp shells, or paper or styrofoam cups can be used.

## Building a Sand Pile

In getting started, the first step is to build up a pile of good, clean, wet sand found near the shoreline. The size of your pile will determine how big a castle you'll be able to build and how much time you'll spend on it. Usually 1 foot of sand is enough for a one-hour sandcastle; likewise a 3-foot-high pile will be sufficient for a three-hour castle. The higher you build your pile, the more sand you will be working with and the longer it will take to sculpt and shape.

Here's a good opportunity to put everybody to work. Everyone can help with the digging and packing. If you're working alone be sure that you pack down the sand with your spade or your foot as you build up the pile. (Figs. 1-1, 1-2, 1-3).

**Fig. 1-1**

**Fig. 1-2**

**Fig. 1-3**

# 2 *The Fantasy Castle*

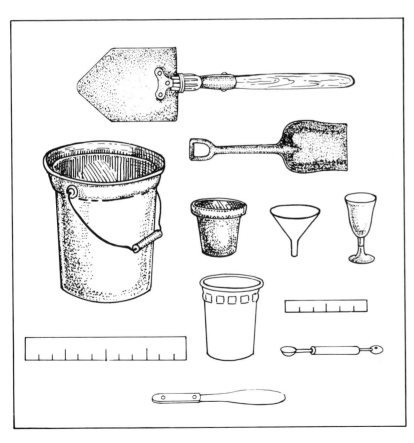

No two sandcastles are alike. The art of building in sand is as limitless as the imagination of the builder. But first you should become familiar and comfortable with the different techniques that can be used in order to build your own castle. If you follow me step by step, then you will be free to improvise and create.

Time: 1 to 6 hours
(depending on your inclination)

Sandcastler's toolbox:
- one large shovel or spade
- one hand shovel
- one plastic beach pail or bucket, 8 to 10 inches in diameter
- one plastic cup, 4 to 6 inches in diameter
- one plastic cup or wineglass, 4 to 6 inches in diameter
- one funnel
- one 6-inch metal or plastic ruler
- one 12-inch metal or plastic ruler or venetian-blind blade
- one spatula
- one melon baller

## The Superstructure

**Step 1.**  With the back of your shovel or spade, flatten the top of a finished sandpile to create a level area about 1½ feet square (Fig. 2-1). This flat area will be used to support the upper structure of the castle.

**Step 2.**  Build two towers on the flat surface. Use the small beach pail as a mold. Pack it firmly with moist sand. If the sand is too dry, it will not hold together. Be sure that the sand is not so wet that it will slide out of the pail. It must hold its shape. Use both hands to pack it, once when it is one quarter filled, again when halfway full, and finally when the pail is completely full (Fig. 2-2).

**Step 3.**  Place your pail upside down on top of the sandpile, sliding it into the proper position. I suggest practicing this step a few times on the beach before actually placing the pail on your pile. You will want to turn the bucket over carefully so that no sand will crumble or slip away.

Once you have tested the firmness of your mold, place it gently on top of the pile. Leave enough room *at the edges* of the pile to prevent your mold from sliding off (Fig. 2-3).

A good way to make sure everything is level is to bend down alongside the pail and check to see if the top edge of the pail is even with the ocean's horizon (Fig. 2-4). Lift the pail up slowly once you are sure the tower will be parallel with the horizon (Fig. 2-5). Repeat this procedure to make the other tower. You should have two firm, compact molds on top of your sandpile.

**Fig. 2-1**

**Fig. 2-2**

**Fig. 2-3**

**Fig. 2-4**

Fig. 2-5

**Step 4.** Now we'll build the foundation for a *bridge* that will span the two towers. Fill in the entire area between the two molds with sand. Take the small hand shovel and scoop up some moist sand from the beach to fill the gap between the tower molds. Pack the sand as you go, using both hands (Fig. 2-6). Fill the entire space, right up against the side of the towers and up to the top of each mold.

I find it easier to carve and shape the towers from molds than from the pile itself. That's why it's best to get the molds in position and then add sand between them for the bridge foundation. If you try to carve out towers from the original pile, leaving sand between each one, you will have a much harder time. A mold is far easier to peel and shape because it is firm, positioned properly, and already close to the shape we will carve.

Now take a spatula and smooth out the top of the bridge foundation so that the surface spanning both molds is even (Fig. 2-7).

Fig. 2-6

Fig. 2-7

**Step 5.** Take a large plastic cup, about 4 to 6 inches in diameter, and pack wet sand into it. Be sure that the plastic cup is smaller than the pail you used to mold your towers. Center the cup upside down on top of one of your two towers. Hold a kitchen spatula across the top of the cup and then turn it upside down. This will prevent the sand from tumbling out of the cup before it is in place. Now set the mold carefully on the left tower and remove the spatula (Figs. 2-8, 2-9). Tap lightly on the top of the cup before you remove it. The sand should hold in the shape of the cup.

**Step 6.** Never clump on the cup! Slowly slide out the spatula. A very light tap on top of the inverted cup will help in removing it, especially if any sand has stuck to the inside walls of the cup (Fig. 2-10).

**Step 7.** You now have two levels. We can go one step higher. This will require a small plastic funnel, about 2 inches in diameter. *A basic principle of engineering a sandcastle is not to put anything heavier on top of a lighter supporting structure.* Fill the funnel with damp sand and turn it over gently on top of the last mold. Use the spatula as a seal for the upside-down cone-shape funnel (Fig. 2-11). Remember to give the funnel a light tap to loosen the sand. Repeat the process on the other tower.

Now, if you have proceeded in this step-by-step manner, you should have added two towers built of three different molds and laid a foundation for your bridge between the two towers.

From this point on 90 percent of your

Fig. 2-8

Fig. 2-9

Fig. 2-10

work will be to carve, shape, and shave the castle out of this form. The first bit of shaping will be the towers.

*A major principle of sandcastling is always to complete your work on a higher level before proceeding to a lower level.* As you carve and shape one level, you will find the excess sand falling and crumbling down upon a lower level. Thus you want to avoid triggering an avalanche on a layer you just spent time developing.

**Fig. 2-11**

**Fig. 2-12**

**Fig. 2-13**

**Step 8.** Now shave some sand away from the cone you created with the funnel. The object is to create a pyramid shape. Take your spatula and make a diagonal cut, grazing through the sand of the cone. When you complete your cut, there will be two edges angling out from the side of the cone. Move to one side and follow this line to make the second sloping side of your small pyramid (Figs. 2-12 and 2-13). Repeat the procedure on the other two sides.

**Step 9.** The bottom of your pyramid forms a square. Follow the lines of this square and use your spatula to shave away the sand on the round mold below the pyramid into a square shape. Grip the spatula at both ends (Fig. 2-14). Shave the sand downward (Fig. 2-15). Shave off a little sand at a time, trying to maintain a vertical direction with your tool. Do all four sides. Repeat Steps 8 and 9 to get the same effect on the second tower.

NOTE:
To create a small ledge on this section of tower, begin your squaring and shaving 1 inch beneath the carved-out pyramid.

**Step 10.** Now to put some windows in your towers: hold the tip of the spatula perpendicular to the ground, so that the edge of the blade will create a vertical slit on the side of the tower (Fig. 2-16). Pull the spatula out toward you, and then make another mark slightly to one side of the previous one. Remove the sand with the tip of the spatula between the two slits you have made in the sand wall. This will create a window (Fig. 2-17). These small, narrow openings should be placed on all four sides of the two square molds beneath each small pyramid.

**Step 11.** Before you create balconies, square off the two longer walls running from the plateau of the main pile up to the surface of the foundation for the bridge. Take a 12-inch ruler, grip it with one hand at either end (Fig. 2-18), and scrape away the sand in a vertical fashion (Fig. 2-19). Continue until the wall is straight and

Fig. 2-14

Fig. 2-15

Fig. 2-16

Fig. 2-17

perpendicular. It should make a 90-degree angle with the flat surface between the two towers. Do this on the ocean side as well, leaving the smaller rounded sides untouched.

**Step 12.** Now you can prepare the side of the tower for a balcony. Cut down about 4 inches of sand wall with the edge of the ruler (Fig. 2-20). This is the first step in preparing this side of the castle for a balcony. In Figure 2-21 you can see that I hold the ruler at either end 1 inch below the edge of the mold to complete the shaving of the sand wall, leaving a 1-inch-wide ledge.

Fig. 2-18

Fig. 2-19

Fig. 2-20

Fig. 2-21

**Fig. 2-22**

**Step 13.** Take your spatula and make the left and right sides of the door in the sand wall. These two marks should be ½ inch apart. Dig out the sand between the two marks to create a doorway with the tip of the spatula (Fig. 2-22). The doorway should be 1½ inches deep. Insert your finger to press in the sides of the doorway (Fig. 2-23). As you slowly remove your finger, press it against the top of the entrance to form an arch. The finished doorway should be ½ inch wide by 1 inch high.

Insert the end of a small ruler under the opening at about a 45-degree angle and dig out a small area of sand at the foot of the doorway. (Fig. 2-24).

**Fig. 2-23**

**Fig. 2-24**

**Fig. 2-25**

**Fig. 2-26**

**Fig. 2-27**

**Fig. 2-28**

**Step 14.** Scalloping is the nicest way to decorate the ledge above the balcony. The finely detailed effect of scalloping will yield small semicircles along the ledge. This step is a lot of fun, because you get to use one of the more unusual sandcastling tools—a melon baller. Just the name itself should prepare you for the joy of scalloping.

Hold the handle of the melon baller so that the little bowl is face down. Ease the cup into the ledge, about ¼ inch from the top. Once it is in place, cut out a small semicircle from the ledge. Scoop out the sand by stroking downward (Fig. 2-25). The cuttings, if they are placed 1 to 1½ inches apart, will create the fine detail around the ledge to make your castle look realistic.

**Step 15.** Now you're ready to finish modeling the balcony. First, draw a vertical guideline down the left side of the balcony. Insert the spatula and move it down the guideline (Fig. 2-26) to create a distinct square side. Be sure not to cut too deeply into the wall. Do the same thing on the opposite side of the balcony (Fig. 2-27). Use the end of the ruler to flick away any sand that remains next to the wall after trimming.

Let's put on the finishing touches to the balcony. First, take the spatula, hold it at both ends horizontally, and place it in the sand wall about 1½ inches below the landing of the balcony (Fig. 2-28). Press it in about ¼ inch and gently pull the spatula straight down. Next, reinsert the spatula ¼ inch below the first cut. Press it in, then down, gently. Do this six or seven times to create a balcony support that looks like an upside-down stairway (Fig. 2-29).

Use the melon baller to scoop out the sand from the center of these inverted steps. Start from the middle of the second indentation and clear out the area down and through the last step (Fig. 2-30).

Congratulations! You've just learned some difficult skills. If it didn't quite work, don't worry. It took me years to refine my technique, and even now the unpredictable cave-in still happens.

**Step 16.** Before we tunnel through the area between the two towers—the final step in completing the superstructure of the imaginary castle—let's put in some more windows and doorways. I like to put a doorway on the side of the wall beneath the balcony (Figs. 2-31 and 2-32). Use your finger and spatula the same way you did when you were making the balcony door. You can put a doorway beneath the other balcony as well and at other strategic positions in the towers. I also suggest putting in five or six windows on the ocean and land sides of the towers.

**Step 17.** Now for the last step. Dig out the tunnel with a hand shovel. First draw an upside-down U in the center of the sand wall between the two towers. Make your marks on both sides. The width of the tunnel should be between 4 and 6 inches. Start with a small hole at the base of the area you have marked out, and then enlarge it slowly.

Use the hand shovel to remove the sand from each end of the tunnel. Gradual

**Fig. 2-29**

**Fig. 2-30**

work from both ends of the tunnel should ensure that the two halves of the tunnel meet. If you neglect one side, you may find that the sand caves in. As you remove the sand and work your way up toward the surface of the bridge, turn the mouth of the shovel over and slowly shave away at the sand. This will loosen it and enable you to scoop it out easily.

You can make the inside walls straight simply by taking the ruler in hand from both ends and working it against each of the inside walls. Move it up and down until the sand is smooth and even. I've learned over the years that a rounded ceiling holds up longer. Leave enough sand at the top of the opening to create an arch. Be careful that you don't dig out the top of the tunnel flush to the bridge.

In the sand that remains at the very top of the opening, make an upside-down V. The ends of the V should run into the walls and meet at the center of the bridge (Fig. 2-33). The extra sand at the joints where the walls of the tunnel meet the bridge should provide the necessary support for the bridge. If you worked slowly and carefully, the tunnel should highlight the bridge and towers.

In the event of a surprise, don't panic. Part of the fun of building a sandcastle is the spontaneity of the project. Unlike real buildings, where a mistake can cost millions of dollars, these mistakes cost you nothing. But you can turn a mistake into an opportunity. Don't go back and try to correct the mistake. Move onward and make the best of the situation. I found, for instance, that the sand around a bridge I made was too dry and knew it wouldn't

Fig. 2-31

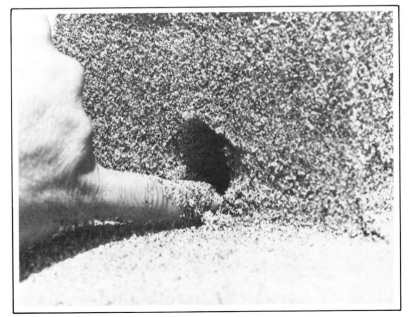

Fig. 2-32

hold for the entire day. Instead of panicking when the bridge collapsed, I cleared away the fallen sand between the base of the two towers. The castle looked equally impressive without it. Because a fantasy castle should be *your* fantasy, you should not repeat my steps every time you go to the beach. Every sandcastle builder has locked in his imagination what he or she wants to build. Your creativity will play a role in all your future castles.

So far you've shaved and carved your molds into two distinct towers. You could stop here and call it a one-hour castle on a hilltop. If you're willing to spend more time, you can create a front wall and stairways to either side of the castle.

## Squaring Off

Most of the work from here on consists of squaring off the pile and adding the staircases. First you make the new walls (Fig. 2-34) and then add the fine details—stairways, windows, and more scalloped ledges.

Here we work down, not up, starting from the plateau on which the towers sit. In order to move down you first have to dig away the sand with a hand shovel. Use the back of the shovel to flatten out the new walls. They should drop *straight* down from the edge of the front back of the plateau that supports the towers. The walls should be at least 8 to 10 inches high. The sand on the balcony sides of the pile that remains will be what you use to build steps.

Fig. 2-33

Fig. 2-34

## Stepping Down

Now you'll learn the secret of "stepping down," or making steps. There are three basic types of steps you will want to master: *regular steps*, *spiral steps*, and *three-sided steps*.

### Regular Steps

These steps, like the others that follow, are done one at a time. I suggest beginning with a set of steps that starts from the doorway beneath the balcony.

Begin at the opening near the doorway (Fig. 2-35). Place a spatula horizontally down into the sand. Cut into the sand about ¼ inch. You'll use the edge of the spatula or ruler to dig and to carve the steps. Now glide the spatula horizontally across the surface of the sand, away from the cut you just made (Fig. 2-36). You should be working the tool to make an L shape. Clear the sand away to create the L. Don't allow the end of the tool to damage the wall. You now have one very sharp and well-defined stair.

Make another L ¼ inch away from the first step by putting the spatula or ruler parallel to the step you just made. Be sure the end of the tool is very close but not into the wall. Again make a cut vertically down into the sand and then move the sand away horizontally. Clear away 4 to 5 inches of sand before you proceed to make the next step. You should now have two perfectly formed, sharp-edged steps. Continue the same procedure until you have six to eight well-defined steps coming down from the doorway beneath the

Fig. 2-35

Fig. 2-36

balcony (Fig. 2-37). For the moment do not be concerned with the sides of the steps. Your primary goal here is to create a stairway that has even and parallel steps. Don't be surprised if at first one or two of your steps are not identical. You will quickly gain the knack of making the steps even.

When you have cut out the number of steps you want, begin to cut away the sand from the right side of your stairway with the 12-inch ruler (Fig. 2-38). Note that you'll be cutting down into a portion of the newly made steps. Hold the ruler flat in order to level and clear the sand away from the side of the stairway (Fig. 2-39). Be careful to maintain a vertical angle when you cut and square the side of your stairs (Fig. 2-40).

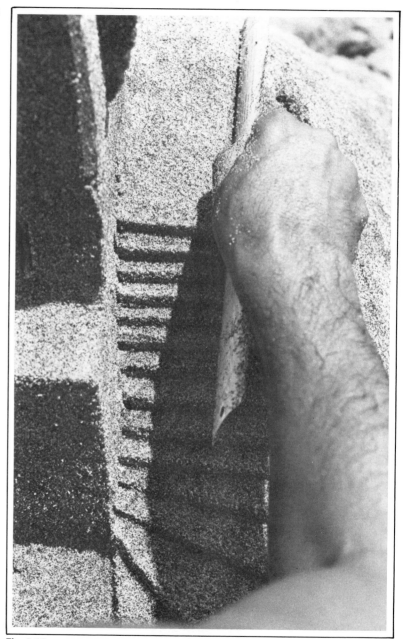

Fig. 2-38

Fig. 2-37

Fig. 2-39

Fig. 2-40

## Spiral Steps

Spiral steps make use of the same techniques used for straight steps. But instead of evenly sized steps, be sure each step is slightly wider than the previous one as you turn the corner (Fig. 2-41). Note how the ruler is eased into the sand ¼ inch and then slid away from the vertical incision to leave a step.

As your steps spiral down to a lower level, prepare the wall for them as you go (Fig. 2-42). Use the hand spade to round off the side of the wall as you start your turn. Picture in your mind how much of a curve you want; then try to visualize that shape in the sand. As you make your curving stairway, see if it corresponds to the image in your mind.

Repeat the same stepping-down procedure from another side, only instead of curving your steps around the corner, try to make them turn at a 45-degree angle away from the side wall. You can try to put in as many of these stairways as you have the time or inclination to do.

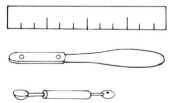

**Fig. 2-41**

**Fig. 2-42**

Fig. 2-44

Fig. 2-43

## Handrails

There is no special trick to making handrails. Rather than holding your spatula or ruler horizontally, hold it vertically (Fig. 2-43). Only the end of the ruler or spatula should penetrate the sand. Place the narrow end of the ruler about ¼ inch into the sand and then horizontally pull the sand away.

When you have reached the bottom of this staircase, use the hand shovel to clear away the sand for your wall and handrail. Cut vertically down with the tool to leave a ledge of sand ½ inch thick or less for the railing. Figure 2-44 shows the finished sculptured handrail and steps.

## Three-Sided Steps

The three-sided stairway you see in Figure 2-45 was built down from the flat landing of the first stairway. The landing was created after dropping down a new section of vertical wall.

Now glance at Figure 2-46. This picture shows the beginning of this new stairway.

Your 12-inch ruler will come in handy now. Hold the ruler on its side and angle off and slide away the sand to make five or six steps out from the center of the landing (Fig. 2-47). Once again you are working the sand in an L-shaped pattern. Make about five or six steps before you stop. These steps should be about 12 inches wide.

Fig. 2-45

Fig. 2-46

Fig. 2-47

**Fig. 2-48**

Work on the sides of each of these wide steps. Each new series of steps from the side will form a right angle to the first step. First use the ruler to clear away a slight incline on each side (Fig. 2-48).

Next place your 6-inch ruler even with the indentations for the first set of wider steps, so that these less wide steps are even with the front and major stairway. The width of each side step will increase as you move down. Square and shave the steps on each side of the stairway so that the three-sided effect is pronounced and sharp (Figs. 2-49 and 2-50). This is the most difficult of the three kinds of stairways and may take a little practice. You can see the result in Figure 2-45.

**Fig. 2-49**

**Fig. 2-50**

## "No-Name" Steps

One more major type of stairway and you will have mastered stepping down. This time dig out another section of front wall toward the left of the three-sided stairway (Fig. 2-51). Use the hand shovel to dig out and square off the section that is visible in the picture.

Hold the hand shovel in the middle of this new level, as illustrated in Figure 2-52. Lay your thumb across the mouth of the tool and continue holding it like this as you make your indentations downward for each step. Again, go into the sand about ¼ inch, pull horizontally, and start again until you have eight or nine evenly defined steps (Fig. 2-53).

**Fig. 2-51**                                    **Fig. 2-52**

**Fig. 2-53**

Now turn the shovel so that its back is flush against the incline of the side of the stairway (Fig. 2-54). Clear away the sand. Use the spatula to peel away any remaining sand so that the side of the railing is straight (Fig. 2-55). Repeat to create the railing on the other side.

Now take a look at Figure 2-56. There's my finished fantasy castle, complete with towers overlooking the ocean and a series of elaborate and detailed steps leading from one level down to the next.

The completed castle, as you can see, has been squared and layered out of the original pile. The basic pattern is always the same—squaring off a section of vertical wall, then stepping down to the next plateau.

**Fig. 2-54**

**Fig. 2-55**

**Fig. 2-56**

## Making Up Your Own Techniques

Making up your own techniques is not difficult. In fact, the more sandcastling you do, the more you will find your imagination taking over. The art of sandcastling is coordinating the mind with the hands. The interplay between the two is endless, and the possibilities are infinite.

One way to discover new sandcastling techniques is to stop in the middle of one of the suggested techniques and let your hands and fingers do whatever they please. Let your hands work the sand in whatever way feels best to them. Use the tools you feel like holding. Don't worry too much about control or artifice. Give free play to your imagination. After all, this is how sandcastling developed. You may find ways to combine parts of the different step-building techniques to construct a whole new type of stairway. Or you may want to use more water on different levels to build pools or free-form structures.

Frequently in the midst of building a wall or tower, something else suggests itself to you. Let your impulse have its say. That's one of the joys of sandcastling. Sand will yield to our whims!

You may even want to learn more about castles. Study their architecture and learn their history and the technical names for their different structures. Then when you build your own castles, you will be familiar with the fine points of historic castles. You might try exploring a few textbooks on castles. Or, if you really become ambitious, you might like to take a course on historic castles.

# 3 *A Lighthouse by the Sea*

The first "lighthouses" were fires lit on the top of a seaside hill or mountain to guide mariners back home into port. Not until the seventeenth century did lighthouses become navigational aids for ships on longer passages and effective warning systems against natural hazards like unseen shoals and offshore cliffs and rocks.

The model for this lighthouse is the Barnegat Lighthouse on the New Jersey shore. For many years it served as a warning that there were treacherous shoals off the coast. Barnegat is a 75-foot-high brick tapering tower with walls 10 feet thick at the base. The last keeper left the small house attached to the tower in 1926. The lighthouse itself is no longer operational because officials decided in 1944 that a lightship offshore would be more effective.

We built our lighthouse on a nearby jetty in order to make it appear more realistic. However, yours can be built on the beach just as well.

The major difficulty of locating a lighthouse on a jetty is the unavailability of sand. You have to carry it to the rocks. A

Time: 1 hour
Sandcastler's toolbox:

- one shovel or spade
- one hand shovel
- one pail or bucket, 8 to 10 inches in diameter
- one plastic wineglass
- one spatula
- one paper or plastic cup

bucket brigade would help, but if one doesn't happen to be available, you'll have to transport the sand yourself. That will take some work. Remember that sand—especially the wet sand needed for sandcastling—can be heavy. Therefore, take your time. Two or three trips should do, using your large buckets (8 to 10 inches in diameter).

**Step 1.**  Choose a flat rock along a jetty and put down a small foundation of wet sand to make a level area about 2 feet square (Fig. 3-1).

**Step 2.**  Now scoop about five spadefuls of damp sand onto the foundation and pack it down. This should form a pancake-size base, which will support three molds piled one on top of the other (Fig. 3-2).

**Step 3.**  Pack your largest bucket with sand and place it squarely atop the base. (Be sure the bucket was filled to the top with sand and leveled off). Tap the bucket to free the sand from its mold, and gently lift the bucket.

**Step 4.**  Strengthen the bond between the base of the lighthouse and the first mold by packing sand uniformly around the base.

**Step 5.**  Now take a medium-size plastic cup, repeat the packing process, and top the cup with sand until it is level and full. Using the spatula to hold the sand in place, set the cup atop the bucket mold. (Fig. 3-3). Be careful! Tap the cup lightly and gently remove it, leaving the mold behind.

**Step 6.**  Finally, pack a plastic wineglass with sand and place it carefully atop the

Fig. 3-1

Fig. 3-2

Fig. 3-3

lighthouse (Fig. 3-4). Use the spatula to keep the sand in place. Tap the mold lightly to free the sand. Be careful not to jar the structure. With the end of the ruler, make a series of vertical markings on the sides of this mold for windows (Fig. 3-5).

**Step 7.** Now the fun begins. First, we'll build a ledge around the top portion of the second mold. A spatula will do for sculpting. Make a line parallel to the circumference of the top of the mold about 1 inch from the top. Using this line as a guide, shave the sand downward at an angle to form an inverted cone (Figs. 3-6 and 3-7).

Fig. 3-4

Fig. 3-5

Fig. 3-6

Fig. 3-7

Fig. 3-8

Fig. 3-9

Fig. 3-10

Fig. 3-11

**Step 8.** Now we'll taper the remainder of the tower. Use a ruler to shave away the sand around the bottom mold down from its top to the foundation (Fig. 3-8), but leave enough sand untouched on one side of the tower near the bottom in order to construct the lightkeeper's house (Fig. 3-9).

**Step 9.** Figure 3-10 shows the small house at the base of the tower. Trace the outline of the roof and the sides of the house in the remaining sand on the side of the tower's base. Then carve the house with the edge of your ruler or spatula. A small doorway can be made in the same way as the one we made in the Fantasy Castle.

I also put a small doorway on the side of the lighthouse tower facing away from the water.

**Step 10.** Finally, hold the ruler horizontally to scrape away the sand that has fallen on the jetty stone (Fig. 3-11). A small hand broom or whisk broom would be effective if one is available.

Now wait for the waves to hit the rocks. This should make a terrific photograph! (Fig. 3-12).

**Fig. 3-12**

# 4 *The Alamo*

Jim Bowie and Davy Crockett were two of the Alamo's legendary defenders. Bowie had been ordered to blow up the Alamo in January of 1836 by Sam Houston, the Texan commander. Houston felt the post was too isolated. Bowie was convinced, however, that the Alamo should be maintained. After all, the fortress was all that stood between the colonists and the Mexicans.

Davy Crockett joined the garrison some time after Jim Bowie with twelve fellow Tennesseans. The total number of "Texans" gathered in the outpost was 183. They were surrounded and outnumbered by 5,000 Mexicans, led by General Santa Anna. The battle lasted thirteen days, and in the end every Texan was dead. But Santa Anna's march into Texas was delayed, allowing General Houston's army time to strengthen forces and resolve.

All that remains of the Alamo today is the chapel wall. This stone masonry building faces west. It is 75 feet long and 62 feet wide. The walls are 4 feet thick and 22½ feet high. Originally the fort had barracks and a large central plaza surrounded on four sides by stone walls.

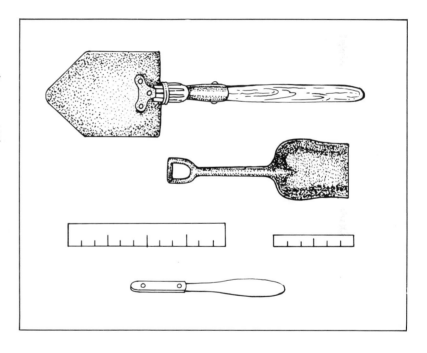

Time: 1 hour
Sandcastler's toolbox:
- one shovel or spade
- one hand shovel
- one 6-inch ruler
- one 12-inch ruler
- one spatula

**Step 1.** All that remains of the Alamo is a chapel wall with a few windows, columns, and a doorway. To build the Alamo, start with a wider pile than you used for the fantasy castle. The pile won't need to be as high because there are no towers. Make the pile about 5 feet wide and about 2 feet high. Use moist sand that packs well.

**Step 2.** Note in Figure 4-1 how the front wall has a small half-circle at its highest point. The most difficult part of building the Alamo in sand is creating the curve at the top of the wall and the sloping walls that move down from its peak. Once you have achieved this effect, the remainder of the wall will be easy. First build up a mound of sand in the center of the front of the pile. Draw a semicircle in the front of

this mound. Take the 12-inch ruler and, with the semicircle as a guide, carve away the sand to create a smooth semicircular shape (Fig. 4-2).

**Step 3.** Now glance at Figure 4-3 to get an idea of the outline of the rest of the top wall. Note that there are three step-like ledges on each side of the dome. Two are located halfway between the top dome and the edge of the building. One is located at the bottom of the dome.

Start at the left-hand side of your pile and draw in the outline of the entire top of the front wall. Now carve away the sand with a ruler, using the guidelines you have just drawn. (Fig. 4-4).

**Step 4.** As illustrated in Figure 4-5, the

most effective way to shape the first wall is to hold the hand shovel in a vertical position. Start at the top of the wall and cut away the sand to create an even surface. Cut down about 6 to 8 inches of sand wall, and remember to leave a ledge 2 to 3 inches wide. The remainder of the vertical wall will drop down from the outer edge of this ledge.

**Step 5.** Smooth out the surface of the ledge by holding the 12-inch ruler horizontally and dragging the edge of the ruler along the ledge (Fig. 4-6).

Fig. 4-1

Fig. 4-2

**Fig. 4-3**

**Fig. 4-4**

**Fig. 4-5**

**Fig. 4-6**

**Step 6.** Now work the top portion of the Alamo wall above the ledge. Your goal will be to carve out one central square window and two arching windows on either side of it (Fig. 4-7).

The method used to make these windows is entirely different from anything you have done thus far. Draw the outline of a 1-inch-wide square in the center of the sand wall directly under the dome, and to either side of it draw a horseshoe that is 1 inch wide at the base.

Hold the 12-inch ruler vertically (Fig. 4-8) and use the edge to scrape away the sand around the edges of the horseshoe. This technique will leave a sharply defined horseshoe-shape arch on the surface of the wall.

Remove the sand from the inside of the horseshoe with the end of a spatula (Fig. 4-9). Flick away the sand from the inner sides of the window. Leave a ½-inch border to create the trim for the window.

**Fig. 4-7**

**Fig. 4-8**

**Fig. 4-9**

Clear away the excess sand that falls on your ledge in front of the window. Trim the base of the window with the spatula (Fig. 4-10).

Follow the same method for carving out the other two windows. Shave away the sand from the outside of the outline and flick away the sand within it to create the effect of a trimmed window.

**Step 7.** Now we're going to square off the bottom of the ledge that will separate the top portion of the Alamo wall from the door and windows beneath it. With the spatula carve out a line 1 inch below and parallel to the top of the ledge. Scrape away about ¼-inch of sand as you go.

**Step 8.** Now it's time to detail and shape the lower section of wall beneath the ledge. Start from the left and put in a pair of columns. Between each column place a long, arching window. Once this work is done, move to the center of the wall to make the entranceway. To the right of this entrance, put another set of columns and another arched window set between them (Fig. 4-11).

**Step 9.** *One of the most important concepts in sandcastling is that you really don't add details. You are merely clearing away sand to make them visible.* All you need to do to make the columns appear is remove excess sand. Notice that the columns run from the ground up to the beginning of the ledge. Do this by putting one hand on the handle of the spatula and glide the blade up against the sand wall with your other hand (Fig. 4-11). Go straight up, keeping the blade tight against the wall. This maneuver will enable you to scrape away the sand in a continuous straight line. Follow this same procedure about ⅜-inch from the side of the mark you just made. There should now be two vertical grooves, running from the base of the wall up to the ledge. The sand that lies between these two grooves should give the appearance of a column.

Fig. 4-10

Fig. 4-11

Fig. 4-12

Fig. 4-13

**Step 10.** To the right of the column, carve out a slender, arching window. Draw the shape of the window in the sand wall and flick away the sand inside the outline. Now make another column. Follow the same procedure described in Step 6 (see Fig. 4-11).

**Step 11.** Draw the outline for the arched doorway directly in the center of the wall, right below the square-shape window in the upper section of wall. Shave away the sand around the edges of the outline with the 6-inch ruler (Fig. 4-12) and flick away the sand inside the outline with your spatula.

**Step 12.** Move down approximately 1 inch to the right and repeat Steps 10 and 11 to build another set of columns; put a window between each one.

**Step 13.** Look again at Figure 4-3 and Figure 4-15. Notice that four more square windows were added to the front wall: two on the right wing, two on the left wing. These were made the same way as the initial square window, which was carved in the upper center of the chapel wall.

**Step 14.** The back wall of the Alamo does not require much attention. You can see in Figure 4-13 that you only have to clear away the sand about 6 inches down from the top of the semicircle at the peak. Leave the rest of the sand behind the wall for support. You can square off the wings with your hand shovel, then smooth down one wall of the wing with the edge of the 12-inch ruler.

# $5$ The Ponte Vecchio

Built around 1345 by Nero di Firnoti, the Ponte Vecchio, or "Old Bridge," spans the Arno River at its narrowest point. It is the oldest standing bridge in Florence, and was the only one not blown up by the Germans as they fled the city in 1944. But what makes the bridge unique is the rows of little houses that line either side of it. Today these houses are occupied by Florentine goldsmiths and jewelers.

The "Old Bridge" is a challenge to make in sand. You'll have fun carving out the little houses, and you'll use the ocean to flood the sand floor beneath the bridge to create the Arno River.

**Step 1.** You'll learn new building techniques when you construct the Ponte Vecchio in sand. Begin by drawing a rectangle in the sand, preferably between the tide line and the water's edge. Make the rectangle about 2 feet wide and 6 or 7 feet long.

**Step 2.** Dig up sand from alongside the rectangle and pile it into the rectangle to a height of 1½ feet. Fill in the entire area. Make sure you keep the height of the pile level. When you finish, there should be a shallow trench on either side of the rectangle.

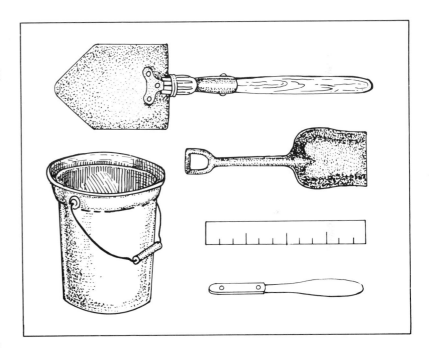

Time: 2 hours
Sandcastler's toolbox:
● one spade or shovel
● one hand shovel
● one spatula
● one 12-inch ruler
● one medium-size pail or bucket

**Step 3.**   Next, draw a line down the center of the top of the pile, from one end to the other. Use the back of the shovel to pat and flatten down the pile on either side of the dividing line to begin forming the roof of the Ponte Vecchio (Fig. 5-1). Create one side of the roof, then the other, so that the two sides meet at the peak.

The roof should be about 5 inches wide on each side. To mark its edges take the spatula and carve an indentation on both sides of the roof approximately 5 inches down from the apex. The lines should run the complete length of the pile. These lines will also serve as the guidelines for squaring off the back side of the bridge and carving out the compartments and arches in the front (Fig. 5-2).

**Fig. 5-1**

**Step 4.**   To square off the back side of the bridge, hold the hand shovel in a vertical position and use the horizontal line you've just drawn as a guide to carve away the sand on the back side of the pile until you have a smooth and even wall. Be sure you leave the roof intact.

**Step 5.**   Now it's time to carve out the structures in the front of the Ponte Vecchio. You'll start on the left-hand side of the front by making four tiers, each a foot long. Building these tiers is like building wide steps. Place a 12-inch ruler horizontally into the side of the wall, press into the sand, then pull the ruler toward you, bulldozing away the sand to leave your first tier. Space each tier an inch apart.

**Fig. 5-2**

Fig. 5-3

Fig. 5-4

**Step 6.** Now put in the small compartments that line the front of the bridge. The unusual thing about these structures is that they lean over the river. At first you might think you have to add something to the sand wall to create the small houses. But just the opposite is true. *Remember that much of the work of a sand sculptor is to free a shape you see in the sand and then remove the excess sand around it.*

Work 3 to 5 inches down from the roof and directly to the sides of the tiers you just created. First, create the angular roofs of the compartments by shaving the sand away with the spatula. Then square off three sides of each compartment. Do this with the spatula by cutting in a vertical motion to clear away the sand (Fig. 5-3). Be sure to smooth off your roofs and walls with the flat side of the spatula to create the esthetic effect you desire.

Put your windows in each compartment. Use the technique outlined in the instructions for the Fantasy Castle.

**Step 7.** Next build a wide ledge in the middle of the front of the bridge. The bottom of this ledge should be continuous with the floor of the compartments. To build the ledge take the hand shovel in the same manner you did for squaring the other side of the bridge. But only cut down as deep as the floor of your houses. Then pull the shovel toward you to clear away the sand. Repeat until you have cleared a ledge 10 to 12 inches long. Smooth down the flat surface of your ledge with the flat side of the spatula (Fig. 5-4). You will be building three archways over this ledge.

**Step 8.** The archways are done by tracing the outline of three horseshoes, 2 to 3 inches wide at their base, in the sand wall. Leave an inch of sand between the outline of each horseshoe. Start by digging out the sand with the tip of your spatula from the bottom of the arch (Fig. 5-5). Now work carefully and slowly to remove 2 to 3 inches of sand. Do not tunnel through. Use your index finger to smooth down the inside walls and roof of each archway.

**Step 9.** After you have carved out all three arches, continue to carve out more compartments along the bridge wall (Fig. 5-6). You may vary the size of each compartment as well as the angle of their roofs. Feel free to make little windows in the compartments of the jewelers.

Fig. 5-5

Fig. 5-6

Fig. 5-7

**Step 10.** Now's the time to square off the sides of the bridge. Start at the left side below the tiers and work your way down the wall. Figure 5-7 shows that the ledge below the archways is of lesser width than the compartments on each side of it. Draw a line in front of the archways, leaving 2 to 3 inches of ledge. Gently carve away the sand to leave a vertical wall.

**Step 11.** The first lower archway should span the width of the three smaller archways above it (Fig. 5-7). This time mark in the sand wall a very wide horseshoe, about 8 to 10 inches. You'll return to it later to tunnel through.

**Step 12.** Now square off the remaining section of the front wall and draw in two more outlines for lower archways, leaving 2 to 3 inches of sand between each one.

Tunneling through all three lower archways is done in a similar manner. Begin digging at the base of each horseshoe with your hand shovel, then switch to the spatula as the going gets more dangerous (Fig. 5-8). Remember to tunnel through gradually from both sides, working from the bottom up and from the center out toward the sides. In Figure 5-9 you can see my hand inside the tunneled area checking that enough sand has been left to support the top of the archway.

**Step 13.** If you are lucky, the tide will creep up slowly so that the ditches beneath the three tunnels fill up gradually. Otherwise you can slowly fill them with ocean water. Be careful not to pour in too much. Molto bene!

**Fig. 5-8**

**Fig. 5-9**

# 6 The Colosseum

*While stands the Colosseum, Rome shall stand. When falls the Colosseum, Rome shall fall. And when Rome falls—the world.*
                                                        —Lord Byron

The building of the Colosseum began in 74 A.D. during the reign of Emperor Vespasian and was completed under the reign of his son, Titus, six years later. Building the Colosseum was quite an engineering feat! The site first had to be drained, since the Colosseum stands where the corrupt Nero once made a royal lake. And a road had to be built to the quarries below Tivoli, where the stone for the Colosseum was cut.

To build the external wall, 292,000 cartloads of travertine stone were used; 750,000 tons of dressed stone, as opposed to unfinished raw materials, were worked into the entire building. To give you an idea of how much stone this is, the Colosseum later provided stone for rebuilding St. Peter's and many Renaissance palaces.

The inaugural games were billed as a great public event. Sixty thousand excited Romans packed the stadium, from the arena floor up to the high rim of the walls. The knights sat in the front row, the senators in the raised balcony above, the emperor and his favorites in the imperial box. The sections that climbed the four-story elliptical structure were first reserved

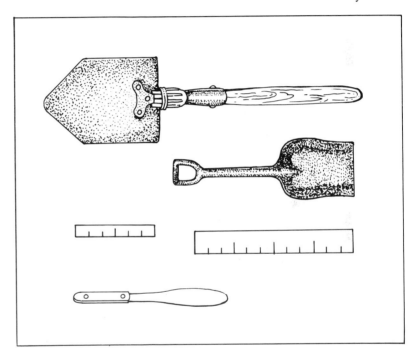

Time: 3 hours
Sandcastler's toolbox:
- one shovel or spade
- one hand shovel
- one spatula
- one 6-inch ruler
- one 12-inch ruler

for distinguished private citizens, then the middle classes, then slaves and foreigners, and finally women and the poor.

Emperor Titus sat proudly in his box. The newly erected stadium was his family's tribute to Imperial Rome. It mirrored Rome's triumph and enthusiasm. No one suspected that four hundred years later the Colosseum would close, and with it the Roman Empire.

The Colosseum's oval arena was 287 feet long and 180 feet wide—the size of a small battlefield, which it was! Onto that field came the gladiators of Rome. The Colosseum stood as a symbol of order and of the power of the imperial government, which fed the public a diet of cruelty and violence. For it was the public who came to the games, and it was the public who

demanded the violence.

Three hundred years passed before the Colosseum's bloodthirsty battles were abolished. The decree came down in 404 A.D. from Emperor Honorius, who had bowed to the wishes of the increased Christian presence in Rome. The Christians had experienced the horrors of the arena directly and had finally gained enough influence to ban the futile bloodshed.

Earthquakes ripped the foundations of the Colosseum in 422 and 508, but it was repaired each time. The ancient monument remained untouched by invaders through the Dark Ages, when it was still the site for wrestling matches and wild animal shows.

By the end of the sixth century, the arena was overgrown with weeds. In 1231 the whole of its southwestern facade

collapsed in an earthquake. But the worst insult came to the structure when in 1590 Pope Sixtus V proposed reconstructing it as a textile factory. He died, however, before he could implement his plan.

**Step 1.** The Colosseum is slightly wider than it is high. Build up the pile about 2 feet and make it about 2½ feet wide. Pack it down as you go (Fig. 6-1).

**Step 2.** It's easier to do the work inside the Colosseum first and leave the more detailed work around the outer walls for last. There are four procedures involved in creating the inside of the arena. The first is to begin to dig out sand from the center of your arena with the hand shovel, leaving enough sand on the insides for the sloping rows of seats (Fig. 6-2).

Fig. 6-1

Fig. 6-2

Fig. 6-3

**Step 3.** The second procedure is to carve out a smaller circle in the center of your Colosseum, which will form the arena floor. Use the back of the hand shovel to flatten and even your floor (Fig. 6-2).

**Step 4.** Now you can build a 1-inch-wide ledge inside the upper rim of the doughnut-shaped pile. In Figure 6-3 you can see that I grip the hand shovel at its neck and cut down vertically 2 to 3 inches of sand from the top of the inner wall. Build this ledge all the way around.

**Step 5.** Now you are ready to put in the benches and rows of seats for the spectators. These will go on the hilly incline that rises from the arena floor up to the ledge you just created.

Hold the hand shovel and place the

Fig. 6-4

Fig. 6-5

mouth of the shovel at the top of this incline (Fig. 6-4). Move the hand shovel as in making an L. This time the indentations should be a little wider, so that each one looks like a row of seats. Work down one section at a time (Fig. 6-5), putting in six to eight rows. Leave some sand between each section of rows. Be careful to make the rows level.

Work your way around the arena to about 2 inches from the arena floor. You should now have a slope on which circular rows of seats are built. It should begin to look like an amphitheater.

**Step 6.** Time for the outside of the arena. Cut away the sand from the top of the outer wall so that you leave a thin wall at

the top, about 1 inch thick. Take the hand shovel and dig the sand away from the rest of the top outer wall (Fig. 6-6). Leave the wall thicker at the base than it is at the top for support (Fig. 6-7). Complete the outer circular wall all the way around and down to the level of the beach.

**Step 7.** Make your markings for three bands of sand that will encircle the outer wall. Each band should be about ½ inch wide all the way around. Do one band at a time, starting with the highest. Use the six inch ruler to mark two parallel lines in the sand wall ½ inch apart that curve around the wall of the Colosseum. Start your first band 2 inches down from the rim of the outer wall. Once your markings are drawn

in, hold the ruler at each end and use it to scrape away the sand beneath and above the area marked for the band.

The result of this work should be a ½-inch-wide band of sand that will stand out from the rest of the wall. Now make another set of parallel lines 2 inches down from your topmost band. Repeat the shaving procedure above and below your lines. Repeat again to make a third circular band.

Fig. 6-6

Fig. 6-7

**Step 8.** This step is the easiest and by far the most fun. I'm sure you remember that a good portion of the Colosseum collapsed in an earthquake. The stone was long ago carried away. The trick to destroying part of your Colosseum is making sure the sand falls away from the outer wall and not down into the arena. Imagine yourself an earthquake and choose a portion of your Colosseum that you wish to demolish. Position yourself outside your Colosseum on the opposite side of this section. Take both hands, palms open and up, and push away about 10 inches' width of sand wall to a depth of about 3 inches.

**Step 9.** All that remains is the detailed work around the outer walls, which will signal to any observer that this is the Colosseum.

Begin by making the famous Roman archways.

Work between the bands of sand you made in Step 7. Begin by drawing an upside-down U figure, or horseshoe in the sand. The archways will be 1 inch wide at the base and, of course, curved at the top.

Take the spatula and place the end of it up against the base of the horseshoe outline. With a gentle flick of the wrist, remove ¾ inch of sand between the sides of the horseshoe. You'll find that if you use the spatula as a shovel to remove the sand, your work will go smoothly (Fig. 6-8).

Build three or four at a time before working down to the next level. In that manner gradually work around most of the wall.

**Fig. 6-8**

Fig. 6-9

Remember as you work down the wall putting in the archways to be careful to put one directly beneath the other. When the sun casts its shadows on the structure, these archways will appear dark, as if all the ghosts of the centuries are lurking there.

Last, tunnel through the uppermost row of arches by working with your spatula from the inside and outside of the wall until you have tunneled an opening.

**Step 10.** If you look at Figure 6-9, you'll notice columns between each archway. The way to design these columns is to carve two vertical grooves in the space between each set of arches. To carve these grooves put one hand on the handle of the spatula and with the other, hold the tip of the blade against the sand wall. Begin to one side of the archway. Now slide that tip up against the wall so you put in a small groove the length of the archway.

Do the same thing 1/8 inch away from the mark you just made. Flatten the sand to either side of these two grooves so that the sand between each of the marks stands out and away from the flat surface of the wall.

Now repeat the process to build a column between each pair of archways. Check to see that the columns are all vertical and, as you move down from one level to another, that columns stand directly over columns.

Don't forget to get a snapshot of the finished work for your photo album (Fig. 6-10).

**Fig. 6-10**

# 7 *The Eiffel Tower*

Do you know that joke about the Eiffel Tower? A Frenchman has his lunch every day on the first floor of the Eiffel Tower. Why? It's the only place in Paris where he doesn't have to look at it.

The Eiffel Tower was built in exactly twenty-six months. Although it was made from 7,000 tons of iron, it used a relatively small amount of metal for such a large structure. If you took all the iron used to build the 1,000-foot tower and made a uniform iron plate covering an area the size of the tower's base, it would only be 6 centimeters thick!

To create the Eiffel Tower in sand, the basic technique is to taper the sides down from the peak. Platforms are then built around each main level of the tower, and by the time you're done you'll have tunneled through the archways at the base. This last step always draws a crowd!

**Step 1.** Pile your sand about 3 feet high. This pile should then be tapered so that it is 3 feet square at the base and narrows to 1 foot square at the top. Flatten down the pile with the back of the hand shovel. Use your hands to smooth down the top of the pile. This flat surface will be the supporting

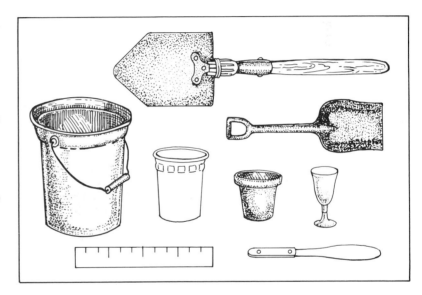

Time: 3 hours

Sandcastler's toolbox:
- one shovel or spade
- one hand shovel
- one plastic pail or bucket, 8 to 10 inches in diameter
- one medium-sized pail or cup
- one plastic wineglass
- one spatula
- one 12-inch ruler
- one flowerpot, 6 to 8 inches in diameter

base for the molds you'll use to create the top of the tower (Fig. 7-1).

**Step 2.** In order to create the illusion of the tower's great height, you will pile up several molds, each one smaller than the next. Pack the plastic 8 to 10 inch beach pail full of damp sand and turn it upside down in the center of the pile (Fig. 7-2). Gently lift off the pail.

**Step 3.** Strengthen the bond between the foundation and your first mold by packing sand uniformly around the bottom third of the mold (Fig. 7-3).

**Step 4.** Use a flowerpot and repeat the packing process. Use a spatula as a lid and turn the flowerpot over on top of the

mold made with the pail (Fig. 7-4). Be sure your molds are straight. Pull out the spatula, rap on top of the pot, and lift it off with both hands slowly and carefully.

**Step 5.** Now make mold number three. Pack the plastic wineglass with damp sand and turn the cup upside down atop the mold you just created with the flowerpot. Voila! This is the top of your Eiffel Tower (Fig. 7-5).

**Step 6.** You'll start tapering at the second mold, the one made with the flowerpot. There are three short procedures. First, square off the second mold to form a four-sided rectangular shape. Then, insert the ruler 1 inch from the top and shave away the sand on all four sides (Fig. 7-6), thus

creating a platform (Fig. 7-8). Third, taper the rectangular shape with the spatula to the point where the next ledge should appear (Figs. 7-7, 7-8). Shave *less* sand from the walls as you go down to the next ledge. Complete all four sides.

**Step 7.** Repeat the procedure in Step 6 to create the next section of tower. One reminder: be sure that as you peel away the sand from each mold the walls gradually slant outward and that they are smooth and continuous. Work slowly and be careful not to peel away too much sand. Your tower should now look like the one in Figure 7-9. Smooth and clear away the sand that may have fallen on the base (Fig. 7-10).

**Fig. 7-1**

**Fig. 7-2**

**Fig. 7-3**

**Fig. 7-4**

**Fig. 7-5**

**Fig. 7-6**

**Fig. 7-7**

**Fig. 7-8**

**Fig. 7-9**

**Step 8.** Now is the time to put in the lattice grid work on the upper sections. Use the end of the spatula to make the crisscross markings as in Figure 7-11. Do this on all four sides, below each platform.

**Step 9.** Create the square platform that supports the tower's upper sections (Fig. 7-12). This is achieved by first drawing a square in the sand at the base of the tower. Leave 2 inches of sand between the bottom of the tower and the sides of the square. Use the outline as a guide and carve 1 inch straight down with the ruler to leave a third platform.

**Step 10.** To create the third main section, you need to dig down into the pile about 1 foot. Use the hand shovel to dig away 1

foot of the sand on all four sides; it should taper to a base wider than the top. Be sure the platform stays intact. I use a ruler to shave the sand so that the resultant sides of this new section will taper outward (Figs. 7-13, 7-14).

**Step 11.** Before we dig down further to create the "legs" of the tower, it's a good time to decorate this new section. In Figure 7-15 note how I press down on the ruler gently to leave two lines, almost vertical and parallel to the outer edge, in the midsection of one side. This creates the appearance of a leg. Connect two lines so the outline looks like an inverted capital U. Peel away ½ inch of sand inside your outline with the end of your ruler (Fig. 7-16). Repeat the same procedure on all four

sides. These figures will create the illusions of openings, especially when the shadows hit them. Mark in your crisscross latticework outside these "openings" (Fig. 7-17). This will simulate the legs of the tower.

**Step 12.** The base of your Eiffel Tower needs to be at least 3 feet wide on each side to prevent it from collapsing. As you dig down to beach level, keep in mind that

Fig. 7-10

Fig. 7-11

Fig. 7-12

Fig. 7-13

Fig. 7-14

Fig. 7-15

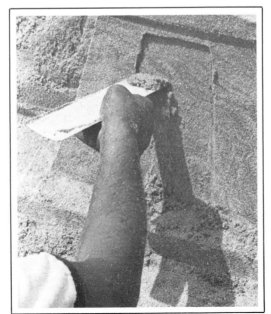

Fig. 7-16

Fig. 7-17

the tower must get wider at its base to support the narrower section above. I suggest you first roughly dig out the base of the tower with the hand shovel and then use the side of the ruler to shave and taper each side of this base. As you shave, begin 1 inch down from the top of each side, just as you did in each previous section, to leave a fourth and final platform.

**Step 13.** Now we'll begin to create the arches on each side of the base of the tower. First, draw an outline of a semicircle on one side of the tower's base (Fig. 7-18). Next begin to remove the sand inside the semicircle with the end of your ruler (Fig. 7-19). Use it like a chisel. Do this on all four sides to create the illusion of four archways. Then put in the lattice grid work to the side of each arch.

**Step 14.** Remember, you'll only want to tunnel through two opposite archways of the tower. If you tunnel through all four archways, too much sand would be removed and the whole tower would collapse.

Tunnel through gradually by carving out the sand inside the semicircle. One technique that will help is to gradually carve out increasingly smaller semicircles as you dig into the sand wall (Fig. 7-20). Always work from the bottom of the semicircle up and from the middle of the semicircle out toward the sides (Fig. 7-21). Clear away the sand bit by bit from two opposing arches until you meet in the middle.

If the sand has been packed tightly, the tower should not collapse.

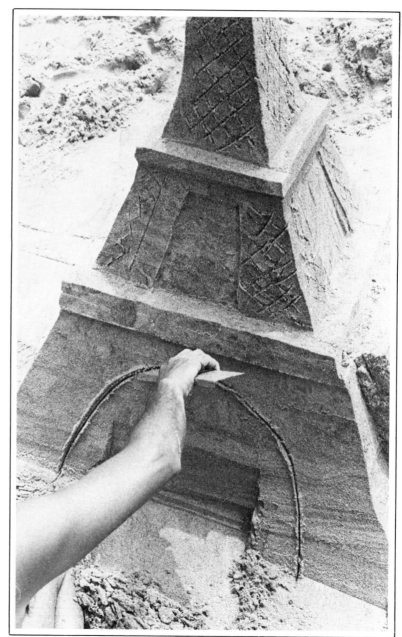

**Fig. 7-18**

Fig. 7-19

Fig. 7-20

Fig. 7-21

# $8$ Great Wall of China

Ancient Chinese legend holds that the first emperor of China's unified Middle Kingdom rode up to the moon on a magic carpet. He didn't like the looks of things—his kingdom seemed too vulnerable. He decided to build a wall around the empire to keep the barbarians out.

The Great Wall of China is the longest construction in the world, stretching about a twentieth of the circumference of the earth. It is the only man-made structure that was visible to the astronauts from their base on the moon.

The Great Wall of China makes a terrific group project. If your group is large enough and has the time, they can build the Great Wall from one end of the beach to the other. A family of four can easily build a 30-foot-long section in two or three hours. It's simple and loads of fun.

**Step 1.** Draw a 15-foot-long S in the sand. A 15-foot-long S section of wall should take a group of four people from one to two hours to build. If your group has more time, draw a second 15-foot-long S so that the two connect and form one long, winding snake (Fig. 8-1).

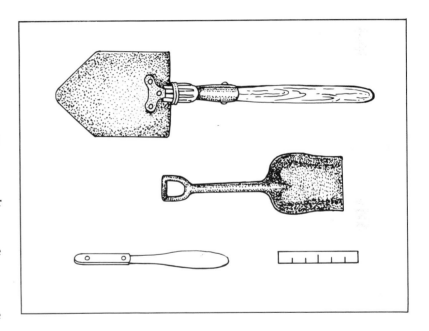

Time: minimum—1 hour
       maximum—all day

Sandcastlers' toolbox:   ● one shovel or spade
                       ● one 6-inch ruler
                       ● one spatula
                       ● one hand shovel

**Step 2.** Pile the sand up on top of your Ss. The resultant snake need only be 1 or 1½ feet high and 1½ feet wide. Pack the length of the pile tightly and flatten the back of it with your shovel, as in each of the other projects.

**Step 3.** Create a road down the center of the pile with the hand shovel. Stand the shovel straight up and, using the mouth of the shovel, bulldoze the road along the top. The width of the road should be between 5 and 7 inches or the width of the mouth of the hand shovel. Level the surface of the road with the back of your hand shovel. Now pack the sand down on either side of your bulldozed path (Fig. 8-2).

**Step 4.** There are a series of notches or small teeth forming battlements that line one side of the Great Wall. You can make these battlements by following three simple procedures.

First, make two short cuts on the side of your wall with your spatula. Space them about 1 inch or so apart (Fig. 8-3).

Fig. 8-1

Fig. 8-2

Fig. 8-3

Next use the end of the ruler to clear out the sand between the cuttings (Fig. 8-4). Finally, use the spatula to trim in half the small rectangles of sand to either side of each notch (Fig. 8-5).

**Step 5.** Create a vertical wall on the side without battlements. Stand the hand shovel straight up and down against the side of the road and cut away the sand vertically so that you clear away the excess from the original pile (Fig. 8-6).

Repeat this procedure on the other side, but be careful to leave the battlements intact (Fig. 8-7). Notice that the width of your original pile becomes narrower and thus leaves a road supported by two vertical walls.

Fig. 8-4

Fig. 8-5

Fig. 8-6

Fig. 8-7

Fig. 8-8

Fig. 8-9

**Step 6.** All that remains to be built are the towers every 5 or 6 feet along either side of the wall (Fig. 8-8). If your wall is 15 feet long, then you should have at least three towers. Likewise, a 30-foot section of wall will have six towers. A good place to build them is where the S bends. The best time to build the towers is after you have built a long section of wall. Make little mounds in the places where you want a tower to go. Draw an outline of the tower's shape in the sand and then cut it out from the mound. Add battlements to the tower walls, and you are done.

When the tide comes in, the first waves will not be strong enough to wash away your work. The aerial view in Figure 8-9 gives you an idea of what the completed section of our wall looks like.

# 9 The Great Pyramid of Giza

The Great Pyramid of Giza in Egypt is one of the seven wonders of the ancient world. Statisticians have figured out that the area of the base could contain the great cathedrals of Florence and Milan, St. Peter's in Rome, and St. Paul's Cathedral in London. If the stones of the Great Pyramid were cut into 1-foot-square blocks and placed end to end, they would extend two thirds of the way around the earth— at the equator!

The Great Pyramid is another ideal group project. If your group is feeling ambitious, they can put in temples, a wall around the pyramid, and one or two smaller pyramids for the king's family.

**Step 1.** Make a pile. The height of your pile will determine the height of your pyramid. The apex of the pyramid will naturally be as high as the highest point of the pile.

This is one of the few times you won't have to pack the sand too tightly. That's because there are no vertical walls to support.

**Step 2.** Take a piece of wood approximately 3 feet long and 6 inches wide and use it to push and flatten down

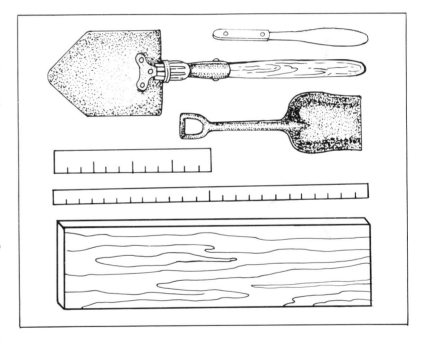

Group project
Time: minimum 3 hours
Sandcastler's toolbox:

- one shovel or spade
- one hand shovel
- one 12-inch ruler
- one yardstick
- one board, 3 feet by 6 inches
- one spatula

the sand on all sides of the pile so they are diagonally shaped, like the sides of a pyramid.

**Step 3.** Carve out at the top of your pile a small pyramidal shape, which will be your guide for carving out the entire pyramid. Use the spatula and cut the sand away in line with the diagonal sides you created using the board. The walls of this small pyramid run from the apex of the pile 10 inches down each side.

**Step 4.** Now take your yardstick and work one side at a time to carve away the sand to create your pyramid shape. Be sure to follow the guide of your little apex pyramid. Remember as you are working that a pyramid is very narrow at the top and very wide at the bottom.

**Step 5.** Once you have reached the ground level on one complete side of the pyramid, start again from the top and go down the opposite side. Stand back and see how your two sides look. You may need to add a little sand to a corner or do some patting down to be sure that the diagonal walls are straight and smooth.

Now work the two unfinished sides in the same manner.

When you have shaved down all four sides, you should have the basic pyramid.

**Step 6.** To create the textured effect of stone, you'll need to make a series of evenly spaced (about an inch or so apart, depending on the scale of your pyramid) horizontal lines from the top of the pyramid down to the base. Make the first

set of lines down from the apex with the edge of the ruler (Fig. 9-1). Apply just enough pressure to make notches in the sand, and work the wider portion of the walls with the yardstick (Fig. 9-2). Again, apply just enough pressure for the horizontal notches. Be careful not to press too hard. Remember to work from the top down. And be careful not to lean against the pyramid.

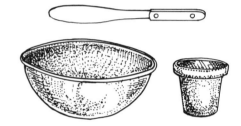

Fig. 9-1

Fig. 9-2

**Step 7.** You will want to put a stairway up to an entranceway on one side. Therefore, don't bother to texturize the bottom of that side of the structure. Begin by tracing the square for a doorway with the end of the spatula about one third of the way up the center of this side. To create the illusion of a doorway, remove about 2 to 3 inches of sand from the outline with the end of the spatula (Fig. 9-3).

**Step 8.** Next, pile up some moist sand to form a ramp leading from the doorway down the side of the pyramid to the beach. Pack down the sand of this ramp with the back of the hand shovel. Use the step method described in the Fantasy Castle section to build a stairway down the ramp to the bottom of the pyramid (Fig. 9-3).

**Fig. 9-3**

**Fig. 9-4**

# 10 The Capitol

*Here, sir, the people govern.* —Anonymous

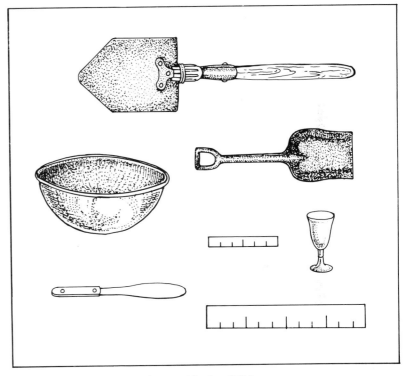

President George Washington laid the first cornerstone for the Capitol in 1793. By 1865 two new wings that accommodated more than five hundred lawmakers were added. In the early 1860s the twin-shelled dome, which weighs nine million tons, was completed. President Lincoln called the work "a sign we intend the Union shall go on." The American sculptor Thomas Crawford's bronze statue, *Armed Freedom*, crowned the dome in 1863. In 1867 new porticoes of the representatives' wing were built.

Over the years the Capitol continued to see modifications and additions. The last major change of the Capitol was initiated in the Eisenhower presidency, when the central area of the Capitol was extended eastward. This new 32½-foot extension added working space and provided a frontal porch for the Great Dome.

The work required to build the Capitol is divided neatly in half. Initially you will sculpt out a three-tiered dome from your pile. The rest of the work will involve carving the front of the building and its fine details: columns, steps, and windows.

**Step 1.** The Capitol requires a very wide pile—a sufficient amount to make the wings of the building. The pile should be approximately 5 feet wide and 3 feet high.

(All-day project when done with the White House)
Time: 4 hours
Sandcastler's toolbox:
- one shovel or spade
- one hand shovel
- one popcorn bowl
- one plastic wineglass with hollow stem
- one 6-inch ruler
- one 12-inch ruler
- one spatula

**Step 2.** There are two good ways to begin shaping a Capitol dome. If you have a popcorn bowl, pack it with damp sand and flip it over on top of the pile. Lift off the bowl and you've got the beginning of the dome. If you don't have a popcorn bowl, build up a mound 1 foot in diameter in the center of the top of the pile. Pat down this mound with your hands so that it is circular, smooth, and firm.

**Step 3.** Next, use a plastic wineglass with a hollow stem as a mold for the statue of *Armed Freedom*. Pack the cup with damp sand. Then place it upside down atop the dome.

The wineglass should leave you with a two-part mold: a protruding end from the stem of the wineglass and a cup-shaped section from the cup of the wineglass.

Narrow the cup section by trimming the sides with a ruler. Use your imagination to sculpt the stem portion of the mold into your *Armed Freedom* (Fig. 10-1).

**Step 4.** Now put in a ring of columns in the cup-shaped mold supporting the statue. This can be done with the edge of a spatula, a small ruler, or, better yet, a small piece of metal the size of a razor blade. The grooves that create the effect of columns go from the base of the statue to the top of the dome. Make vertical strokes with the edge of your cutting tool ¼ inch into the sand. Space the grooves ¼ inch apart. The remaining sand will stand out as columns.

**Step 5.** The completed dome is tiered like a wedding cake. To achieve this effect you have to carve out the tiers of the "cake"

one by one from the pile.

The second tier should be 1 inch wider than the base of the dome's roof. Draw a circle with your ruler around its base, leaving 1 inch between the edge of the dome and your circle. This will be the guideline for cutting away the sand to make the second tier. Begin by holding the hand shovel straight up and down, and carve down along the guideline 6 inches to leave a 6-inch-high circular wall of sand.

**Step 6.** Trace another line 1 inch down from the top of the new wall all the way around it, and then smooth and even the surface of the wall below that line. Use your spatula or the side of your ruler to scrape away gently and uniformly about ½ inch of sand all the way around this second tier (Fig. 10-2).

Fig. 10-1

Fig. 10-2

**Step 7.** Now we'll put in another set of columns around this tier. These grooves should be spaced ¾ inch apart. Use the edge of the 6-inch ruler to make your strokes and to dig out the grooves (Fig. 10-3). Each stroke will run from the bottom of the tier to 1 inch below the top of the tier.

Remember, the sand that lies between each set of grooves should stand out as a single column. You may need to clean out your grooves with the tip of a fine tool so that the columns clearly stand out. Because you're working on a round structure, plan ahead so that when you come to the end of making the columns, they are all properly spaced.

**Step 8.** To carve the third tier repeat the instructions for the second tier. This tier should drop 10 inches and be 1 inch wider than the previous tier.

Put in the columns the way you did on the previous tier. These will be slightly longer but still should be spaced about ¾ inch apart. From time to time step back to see that the columns are straight and evenly spaced.

**Step 9.** Now cut out a hexagonal (eight-sided) platform for the three-tiered upper section of the Capitol. Grip the ruler at either end and make eight clean cuts, each about 5 or 6 inches long, around the base of sand of this upper section (Fig. 10-4).

**Step 10.** The first half of your work is done. Now it's time to carve out the rectangular ground floor of the building. Be sure you leave a flat surface of sand (8 to 10 inches) directly in front of the dome.

**Fig. 10-3**

**Fig. 10-4**

Fig. 10-5

Fig. 10-6

Fig. 10-7

Fig. 10-8

The width of your rectangle can extend out to the sides of the pile.

Figure 10-5 presents a completed shot of the front of the building. Although it may look difficult, you can easily make use of techniques you have already learned to achieve this effect.

**Step 11.** We'll begin by building the three triangular roofs. Then we'll carve out the windows and columns, and last we'll put in our steps.

Build up three small piles of sand on top of the rectangular cutout—one in front of the dome and two more on either side. These will become the wings of the building. Now look at Figure 10-6 and study the inverted squat of these roofs. Trace in the mound of sand the outline of each roof, and then cut away the figure with the spatula.

**Step 12.** Each roof covers an entranceway with columns and steps. To make the columns use the edge of a smaller tool (Fig. 10-7). Space the grooves ¼ inch apart in the sand below each roof. The result should be three sets of vertical columns, each set about 8 inches across. To the sides of each set of columns, trace in outlines of square windows. Then flick away the sand inside each outline with the tip of the spatula.

**Step 13.** Now it's time to step down. The largest staircase runs directly up to the central entrance. This set should be done with the 12-inch ruler, following the stairs method used in the Fantasy Castle. Be sure

to leave sand on either side of the stairway to square off 1-inch-wide railings (Fig. 10-8).

Use the 6-inch ruler to build a set of three-sided steps down from the columns on each wing (Fig. 10-9). These steps get wider as they descend.

In my example I got carried away and made additional steps, but you don't have to (Fig. 10-10).

**Fig. 10-9**

**Fig. 10-10**

# 11 The White House

The planners of the White House held an open competition for designs. The winner, James Hoban, submitted a plan that called for a three-story boxlike structure that could easily be expanded by adding wings at both ends. President Washington was a great supporter of the construction and helped the project over many obstacles, but when he left the Capitol for Mt. Vernon in 1797, the house was incomplete. President John Adams was the first to set up residence there. When he first laid eyes on the site on November 1, 1800, he saw shacks and rubble on the grounds and unfinished rooms inside. That evening he wrote to his wife: "I pray Heaven to bestow the best of Blessings on this House and all that shall hereafter inhabit it. May none but honest and wise men ever rule under this roof."

The White House does not have as much detail as the Capitol, and it is not nearly as high. You'll begin as you do for every other castle—with a pile. You will do some simple carving to get the shape of the house, and then add the portico (a row of columns supporting the roof to the entrance of the building).

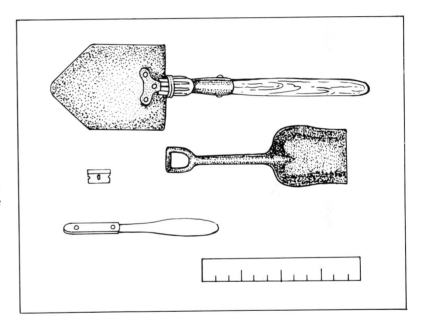

Time: 3 to 4 hours

Sandcastler's toolbox:
- one shovel or spade
- one hand shovel
- one 12-inch ruler
- one small piece of metal (a razor blade will do)
- one spatula

**Step 1.** Because the White House is one of the lowest structures you will build, you need only build a pile 4 feet wide and 2 feet high, in the shape of a rectangle. Flatten the top of this pile with the back of the shovel. Add extra sand to the middle of the front wall to create a hump. This will eventually become the front entrance of the White House.

**Step 2.** Now trace the lines of a rectangle 3 feet long and 1 foot wide on top of the pile. This rectangle will form the outline of the roof of the White House.

**Step 3.** Holding the shovel straight up, scrape away about an inch of sand from the area inside the rectangle (Fig. 11-1). You can see how to even the vertical sides of the ledge by holding the back of the shovel flush against the edges of the wall (Fig. 11-2). Gently scrape across the rectangle to create an even and smooth surface.

**Step 4.** Create two chimneys on the roof by making two little mounds of sand on both sides of the rectangle. Cut out a square shape from each mound with the spatula to get the chimneys (Fig. 11-3).

**Step 5.** The next architectural feature requires creation of a ledge or railing around the rectangle. To do this we need to remove the sand in an even manner from all sides of the rectangle. Hold the ruler at both ends and cut into the sand 1 inch along each side of the rectangle. In Figure 11-4 you can see how I have used the ruler to leave a small ledge on all four

Fig. 11-1

Fig. 11-2

Fig. 11-3

Fig. 11-4

sides of the rectangle. Use the ruler to create this ledge. In these pictures you can also see the front hump of sand mentioned in Step 1.

**Step 6.** Now draw a semicircle on the top of the hump. This will be your guide for carving out the circular front of the White House.

**Step 7.** Next take the hand shovel or 12-inch ruler and carefully carve away the sand wall following the outline of the semicircle (Fig. 11-5). Carve three quarters of the way down the pile, leaving the bottom quarter unsculpted.

**Step 8.** Now leave the front and attend to the sides of the building. Look at Figure 11-6. On the right you can see me working with the hand shovel to square off a wing. On the left side you can see the finished wing. And in the front you can see how much sand I have carved for the front entrance.

**Step 9.** Take the hand shovel and carve out from your pile an extension that begins a quarter of the way down from the top of the roof, and then smooth off the top of your extension with the back of the hand shovel.

**Step 10.** Draw a guide for shaping the wing. The wing will be 5 inches wide. It will be flush to the back of the building and set back 2 or 3 inches from the front of the building. Draw an outline on the top of the extension for these dimensions and use the shovel and ruler to carve out your wing. Repeat for other wing.

**Fig. 11-5**

**Fig. 11-6**

Fig. 11-7

**Step 11.** Once you have your East and West wings, it's time to put in columns. There will be four columns on each side. We create these columns by making four vertical grooves ¾ inch apart. Move the corner edge of the ruler straight up and down against the sand wall (Fig. 11-7) to leave each groove. Dig out any loose sand from the groove with the corner edge of the cutting instrument. The sand between these grooves will stand out as columns. Repeat this process on the sides of each of the wings.

**Step 12.** Glance at Figure 11-8. That's about where you should be. In this picture you can see two protruding ledges along the top of the semicircular front entrance. You can create this effect by drawing in a line 1 inch down from the top of the landing and shaving ½ inch of sand away under that line (Fig. 11-9). Then make a line 1 inch below the ledge you just made and shave the sand another ½ inch deep along the sand wall. Now you've got two ledges.

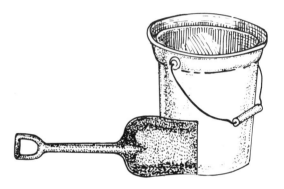

Fig. 11-8

Fig. 11-9

**Step 13.** Create seven or eight columns along the front (Fig. 11-10). Each column is spaced ¾ to 1 inch apart. Scrape out a groove by using the small edge of the ruler. Note that these grooves are wider than the grooves on the wings of the building. Start at the bottom and scrape and then dig out your groove up to the lower ledge (Fig. 11-11). Use the edge of a small piece of metal to smooth and clean out each groove (Fig. 11-12). Make nine such grooves for eight columns. Remember, the sand between each pair of grooves stands out as a single column.

Fig. 11-10

Fig. 11-11

Fig. 11-12

**Step 14.**   Now we need to make two rows of windows on the main building. Make four windows on each wing and twelve windows on the front, six on the left and six on the right. To make these windows trace a rectangular outline for each window and then scoop out the sand from your rectangle with the tip of the spatula or any small piece of metal (Fig. 11-13).

**Step 15.**   Glance at Figure 11-14. Hold the ruler at both ends and do your carving 1 inch out from the columns. Follow the semicircle around as you trim this lower portion of the front entrance. You will make six or seven arches in this smooth section of front wall.

Each arch will be horseshoe-shaped (Fig. 11-15). Make them 1 inch or more apart. First draw an outline of the horseshoe and then dig out the sand from your outline with the flat end of the spatula, going about ¾ inch into the sand wall. Make six or seven arches around this lower section.

**Fig. 11-13**

**Fig. 11-14**

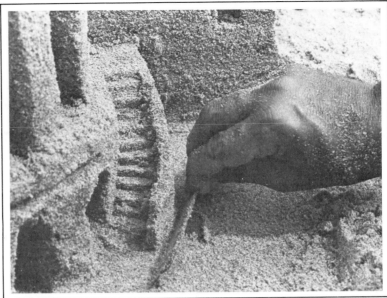

Fig. 11-15                                              Fig. 11-16

**Step 16.** There is a curving stairway alongside the front entrance of the White House. Make yours by building up a small incline of sand alongside the entranceway. Then hold the 6-inch ruler straight up and down at the top of this incline. Dig in ⅛ inch and push the sand away to get your first step. (See stairs in Fantasy Castle.) Repeat to build eight or ten steps that curve slightly against the wall (Fig. 11-16). Square off a side railing for this stairway with the back of the hand shovel.

**Step 17.** Figure 11-16 shows the base of the stairway being swept clean and Figure 11-17 shows the completed White House.

Fig. 11-17

# *12* *Sand Drippings*

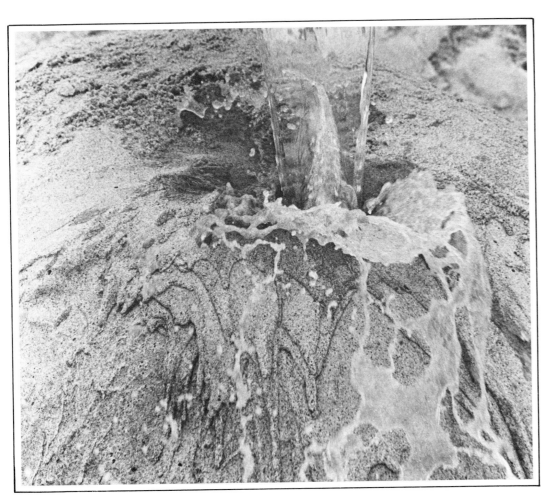

Dripping a sandcastle violates our first principle: working from the top down. The only way you can drip a sandcastle is from the bottom up.

Another difference you'll notice right off the bat is that sand-dripped castles require no pile. Those of you who may be tired of digging will sigh in relief. Occasionally some "drippers" will begin their work on a small pile, so that there is some height already built into the structure. But the majority of dripped sandcastles begin right down on the beach.

Another significant change will be the absence of all the fine detail work required for the other structures. Dripped castles do not need cutting and shaving or squaring and stepping down. Therefore, you won't need as many tools. All you really need to bring along is a medium-size beach pail.

Dripping a sandcastle is the simplest form of sand architecture. If you walk down the beach on any summer Sunday afternoon, you'll find that almost half the people building sandcastles are using the drip method. That's because it's the one most children learn from their parents.

The first step is to fill up your beach pail with water. Wade into your favorite ocean and let the salty water fill your pail.

Be careful! No jellyfish, no seaweed, no small fish—all these will cause technical difficulties.

Next, fill half your bucket with good damp sand, the kind we've been using all along to build our castles. Here, again, watch out for unwanted elements— seaweed, shells, pebbles, and sand crabs. The finer the sand, the less trouble you'll have. If the sand in your bucket is grainy and rough, it will not drip easily into castle form. The sand will simply not adhere. The best sands for dripping are the brown sands you find on most beaches. One expert reports that white coral sand is not satisfactory for dripping because it does not stick to itself easily enough.

Now reach through the water and pick up a fistful of sand. Your fist will function as a funnel. Loosen your fist slightly and hold your thumb on the top. You can open the bottom of the funnel by loosening your little finger so that the sand drips out in a stream. If you find that the sand squirts out in lumps, then your sand is not the right consistency.

The shape and architecture of your dripped castle is entirely up to you. You can do almost anything with dripped castles—leaning towers, zigzag towers, or futuristic cities. The two small boys in Figure 12-1 have dripped three small towers on top of a small hill. In Figure 12-2 you can see them doing an offshoot of the first method. In these pictures they simply hold their two hands together, relax them slightly so that an opening forms between their two hands, and let the wet sand run through the crack.

**Fig. 12-1**

**Fig. 12-2**

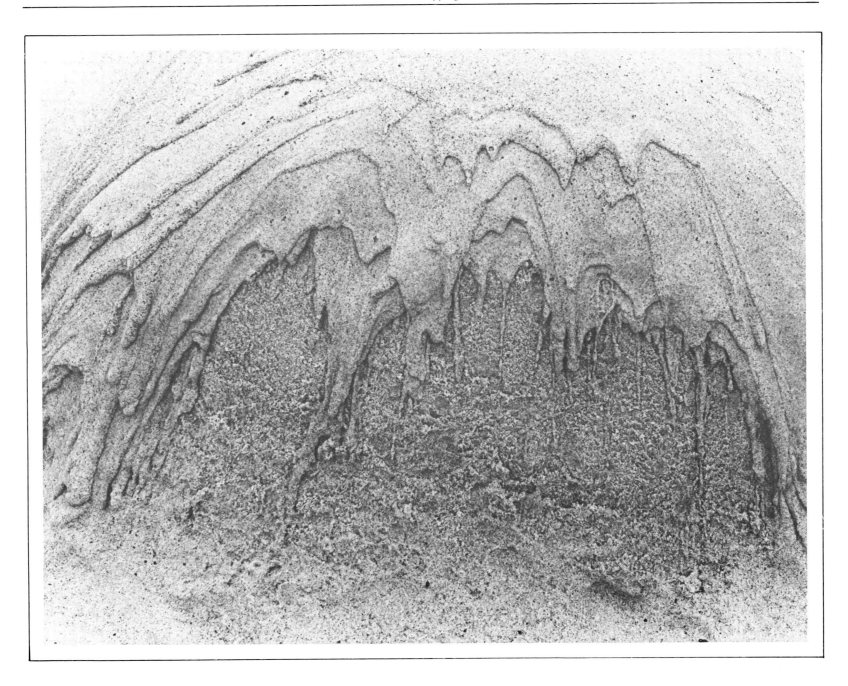

# 13 *Photographing Sandcastles*

Building a sandcastle is like having money in the bank: you can't take it with you when you go. Sooner or later all that beach sand you worked at for so long to build into your castle becomes part of the beach again. Of course, you do want to be certain that if you're going to spend hours sculpting a sandcastle, the photos you take don't make it look like a meager facsimile of the real thing.

If they are done properly, your photos can picture your sandcastle with the same degree of imagination and skill that you used to build it. A good picture can make your sandcastle look majestic, mysterious, triumphant, three-dimensional, even larger than it actually was.

How do you take good pictures of your sandcastle? Three factors influence the finished product:
1. the angle you select to photograph your sandcastle;
2. the elements you use to compose your photograph;
3. the proper lighting.

But before we begin to talk about these three elements, let's talk for a moment about film and cameras.

Beach conditions require film that will adapt well to bright, highly reflectant outdoor conditions. You might keep that in mind when you drop by your local photo store. If you're uncertain, ask the clerk for guidance. With the availability of cameras that process the photos right before your eyes, you have still another choice to make: whether to use a Polaroid process camera.

If you expect to get really interesting pictures of your sandcastle, you have to have a camera that employs film that can be enlarged inexpensively. That means that you're better off leaving your Polaroid process camera at home when you go to the beach. The reason is that those little three-by-three photos you get from a Polaroid process camera just don't have the right impact for sandcastles.

For that reason, if you're going to bring an inexpensive camera to the beach, you're probably better off with an Instamatic-type camera, because it is a simple and inexpensive process to take your negatives to the camera store and have your pictures "blown up" to the size at which you get a sense of the size and detail that made your sandcastle the miracle of architecture that it was.

A high-quality, expensive camera can do the same things and do them better; but an expensive camera can present the sandcastle builder with problems. For one thing, sand is the chief enemy of any finely crafted instrument, which is exactly what a good camera is. And if you've been to the beach recently, you know how the sand finds its way into everything. Second, the newer cameras, which are all electronic, are especially sensitive to moisture. If you accidentally get an electronic camera wet—particularly with saltwater—there isn't much you can do except buy a new camera.

## Angle, Composition, and Light

There are two nice things about taking pictures of sandcastles: you don't have to tell them to stand still, and you don't have to ask them to say "cheese." On the other hand, you can't blame any bad pictures on the sandcastle. So if you expect to take good pictures of your sandcastle, you'll have to follow a few simple rules.

*Angle.* When we talk about angle, we're talking about the direction you want to aim your camera when you snap your picture. Basically there are three angles: high, low, and level.

A high angle gives you an aerial view of your castle. A high angle can work to your advantage if you're building a tall, angular structure. Generally, however, these high-angle shots make the sandcastle look small. Instead of making the castle stand out, they tend to diminish the castle.

Taking the picture straight on usually doesn't work, either. It tends to make the

castle look flat and two-dimensional. The pictures generally appear amateurish and uninteresting. However, a low-angle shot of a sandcastle is different and produces exciting results. Getting down on the beach and pointing the camera up at the sandcastle makes it appear larger than it is. It appears to loom up like the real thing. And if you think about it, most castles were built on hilltops or redoubts in order to make them more defensible. We're accustomed to looking up at real castles; photographs of sandcastles taken from a low angle appear more natural.

*Composition.* It's actually hard to separate "angle" and "composition" when you talk about picture taking. But here when we talk about composition, we're talking about all the things you're going to put in the frame when you take your picture.

Do you want to put your family or friends in the picture? Do you want to show the castle by itself? Are you trying to create a mood or capture details? All these are considerations you should keep in mind when you prepare to photograph your sandcastle.

If you want to photograph your friends and family with your sandcastle, it's generally best to have them pose behind the castle. Also, it's a good idea if they can squat down or sit on their knees for the picture, so that they won't overwhelm the castle. Remember, the reason for the picture is the sandcastle, and if you want it to stand out, it has to occupy a position of importance in the frame.

Action is another important element in composing your photograph. You might want to have someone take your picture as you work on the sandcastle.

The thing to be most aware of when you photograph your sandcastle is the background. Don't clutter up the background by standing too far from your sandcastle when you take the picture. Also, when you look at the castle through the camera's viewfinder, make certain that there's nothing in the background (a stray shovel, passerby, etc.) that distracts from the sandcastle.

At the same time you must be careful not to sacrifice perspective. If you picture the castle all by itself, it's difficult to tell how large or small it is. The answer is to include someone in the picture for perspective, but to pose the person in such a way that he or she doesn't overwhelm the castle.

Another important consideration is detail. Be on the lookout for interesting details. For example, if you built a nice set of stairs coming down from the balconies, select a suitable and impressive angle and snap a picture. Get as close as possible while keeping your camera in focus. Try taking pictures from several different angles. You'll be surprised by the effect.

*Light.* The final and perhaps most important consideration in photographing your sandcastle is light.

Whether you're using color film or black-and-white film, the angle at which the light strikes your castle is important. With the sun high overhead, the light falling on your sandcastle can make it look flat and one-dimensional.

The best time to begin taking pictures of your sandcastle is late in the day, after noon, when the sun is lower in the sky and casting nice long shadows. It is those shadows that make the details of your sandcastle stand out.

If you're using color film (which I recommend), then you should know something about what professional photographers refer to as the magic hour, which is usually the hour around the time the sun rises or sets. It is during that time that the color of the light is especially beautiful. Mornings near the ocean tend to have a blue-green cast, and evenings near the ocean tend to have a red-gold cast. While most of us don't notice the changing color of light, the color film in your camera does. In order to display the deep gold color hidden in the sands of your castle, the best time to take your photographs is toward evening, when the long shadows of the low sun trace dark trails down the beach.

# 14 *How to Enter a Sandcastle Contest*

There is no official bulletin, no sandcastlers' newsletter, so you have to find out about many of the smaller contests by word of mouth. Occasionally a sandcastle contest may be announced in a local newspaper or a sign will go up on a lifeguard stand or a community bulletin board. The bigger events have gained a reputation over the years and are often publicized on radio and television.

At Mission Beach in San Diego, it's not uncommon for a few hundred thousand people to gather to watch the modern wizards of sand. One of the bigger events of the summer on the East Coast occurs in late August out on Steep Hill Beach in Ipswich, Mass. It attracts several thousand people annually.

If you get to a contest early enough, you'll see the teams of castlers piling out of their cars carrying their own special tools: rulers or tape measures, spatulas, and melon ballers. Keep an eye out for the proud solo builder who walks down to the beach silently, all his tools stashed away in a single green beach pail. He may be the type who will work diligently for the next six hours and knock your socks off with a seven-story castle.

Once a contest begins, the crowd splits into two main groups: the spectators and the builders. It's great to be a spectator! You can use the event as an excuse to deepen your tan or to perfect your own castling techniques by watching the contestants. You may even find yourself cheering for a particular sculpture.

The builders, on the other hand, usually spend their time in more frenzied activity. There are judges to please, molds to add, ledges to carve, and only limited time to do it all. Teams of contestants divide the responsibilities quickly once the contest has begun. Some prepare the molds. Others fit them into place. Still others add the fine details. Signs of nervousness increase in the last hour, when they've still got to add the trunk to an elephant or finish the "legs" of the Eiffel Tower.

Things to remember about sandcastle contests:

*Preparation.* Because the contests are competitive, it's always best to practice beforehand. You may have a number of different structures in your sand grab bag. Find one that draws a crowd. Then perfect it. Try building it at least three or four times before the competition.

We don't want to make it sound like you have to be a professional to enter a contest. Most sandcastle contests do have many categories for participants, but if you plan to work on a high level, then you will need to practice.

*Registration and fees.* Most of the contests you enter will have registration on the day of the contest. There will be a registration table set up on the beach. The fees vary, depending on the contest. The Ipswich affair charged eight dollars for all-day parking, but that fee covered entering the contest as well. Promotional events may be "freebies." The Golden Nugget Casino sponsors an annual free contest at Atlantic City, New Jersey. All the contestants receive Golden Nugget Sandcastle T-shirts. Many smaller affairs sponsored by local community recreational groups are free. Check beforehand to know what you are getting into. Naturally those contests with higher fees will have the best prizes. But nobody gets rich entering sandcastle contests. It's not like the PGA, where each week thousands of dollars hang on a putt. A misplaced window or a collapsing tower may cost you something in the eyes of the judges, but you don't have to worry that your pocketbook will be jeopardized.

*Categories.* Each contest will establish its own. One contest may prefer group activities to solo flights; another will emphasize sand creatures and sculptures as opposed to sandcastles. Most contests, however, will accommodate a wide variety of activities, age groups, and working arrangements.

The judges at the Golden Nugget contest, for example, established two major

categories—sandcastles and sand sculptures—and prizes were awarded for group and individual efforts.

At the Ipswich contest things ran a little differently. Although the judges also divided the work into castles and sculptures, there were four different categories for contestants. Professional designers worked in their own league, families in their own bracket, and kids under eleven in still another. Whoever didn't fit into one of those three categories was placed in the "none of the above" category.

*Time Limits.* You will have anywhere from four to six hours to finish an entry. That's enough time to finish any of the structures in this book.

One tip to remember is to dig up your pile quickly. Judges look for details in contests, and you want to leave yourself plenty of time to add all the right crowd-pleasing touches. Since valuable time can be wasted digging up your pile, try to get it done as quickly as possible.

*Location.* Try to find a good level spot on the beach. One of the problems of building at a contest is that there is a shortage of good space. If you are really keen, come to the beach a day before to get the lay of the land. Look for a good level area, one where the sand is not too grainy or rough. Then on the morning of the contest, position yourself early so you can quickly get to your chosen spot.

*The Judges' Scorecard.* You can spot a judge if he or she comes up to your castle, scrutinizes it, and then jots down some figures on a pad of paper before walking silently along. The judge may appear by your side an hour or two into your work,

and then you might not see him again until the last hour of the contest. Consider yourself lucky if in that last hour he stops to pause to look over your shoulder or kneels down to inspect a stairway or the scalloping on a ledge. That means he is seriously interested.

Most contests will assign separate judges for castles and sand sculptures. At the Golden Nugget, for example, a local sculptor judged the sand creatures and other sculptures, while a castler of great renown judged the castles.

One caution: don't let the judges upset you. Contests are supposed to be fun, and by the end of the day, the ocean treats every piece of work the same. So give it your best shot and have laughs along the way.

What do judges look for? We asked one judge what qualities most impressed him. His reply: "Design, imagination, fine detail."

## Design

"Design" refers to the overall conception of your work. Even the most fantastic fantasy castle should have some design to it. Every feature need not be perfect, but the overall effect should be harmonious. Stand back from your work from time to time and ask yourself if the overall picture is pleasing or if the work appears chaotic. If the castle is pleasing, no matter how unusual or far out it may be, then the chances are there will be some design to it.

## Imagination

"Imagination" is tough to define. Writers and artists have been trying to pin it down

for centuries. We like to think of it in connection with creativity. If you pack a beach pail up with sand, and turn it over on the beach, you are left with a mold. If it is left alone, your mold won't look like much. It lacks imagination. But if you dig a moat around it, the whole picture changes. It becomes more interesting. Sculpt a tower out from your mold, and still more creativity is expressed. The more fine details, the more surprises your castle offers, the more imagination you will express.

## Fine Details

Judges like fine details because they reflect craft and patience. Besides, it's the fine details that can really make an authentic-looking castle. It's a good idea to make windows rather than leave the walls of your towers empty. Scalloped ledges are better than plain ledges. Finely built stairways always impress, and a well-placed balcony might just win you a blue ribbon.

## Entry Suggestions

All the castles in this book are winners! The Eiffel Tower is especially good because of its great height. Once you have mastered the technique of building up molds for great height and have tapered the sides of the tower enough times so that from a distance the tower is graceful, you will be ready to enter it in a contest. The judges can't help but be impressed by the size of the tower, the archways at the base, and the fine details, like the tower's platforms and lattice gridwork.

The Capitol is a sure winner. No other sand structure we know of has quite so much detail. Remember, the dome itself has

three sets of columns around each tier. You can create elaborate stairways down the front of the building that are guaranteed to impress the most critical observer.

Last, the Colosseum will have great popular appeal. Each time we have seen it done, this ancient arena attracts photographers from up and down the beach. That's because the archways can be made so realistically, the inside of the arena so impressively, and the collapsed side of the Colosseum so convincingly.

## Prizes

The biggest prize of all is just the fun that goes along with a day of sandcastle building. Of course, you don't have to enter a contest to have fun. Maybe you will win a free weekend at a resort. For its grand prize the Golden Nugget awards a free weekend for two at the Atlantic City Hotel. Second- and third-place winners received a cement-and-sand replica of a castle with an attached plaque. Everyone comes away with a ribbon and a T-shirt.

The winning castles may find their way into newspapers or magazines. A giant lobster that was spray-painted red at Ipswich was photographyed for *Time* magazine. Anything can happen!

**Michael Dipersio** lives in Bradley Beach on the New Jersey seashore and has built hundreds of castles from Massachusetts to Delaware. A master castler, he built his first sand castle in 1969 for his daughter.